SUPERMOTO
ALL-AROUND SKILL AND SPEED

BY LISA J. AMSTUTZ

CAPSTONE PRESS
a capstone imprint

Published by Capstone Press, an imprint of Capstone
1710 Roe Crest Drive, North Mankato, Minnesota 56003
capstonepub.com

Copyright © 2026 by Capstone. All rights reserved. No part of this publication may be reproduced in whole or in part, or stored in a retrieval system, or transmitted in any form or by any means, electronic, mechanical, photocopying, recording, or otherwise, without written permission of the publisher.

Library of Congress Cataloging-in-Publication Data
Names: Amstutz, Lisa J., author.
Title: Supermoto : all-around skill and speed / by Lisa J. Amstutz.
Description: North Mankato, Minnesota : Capstone Press, [2026] | Series: Dirt bike blast | Includes bibliographical references and index. | Audience: Ages 9-11 | Audience: Grades 4-6 | Summary: "The supermoto bikes twist around a paved track. Reaching the dirt section, they catch air over jumps. Supermoto racers put their skills to the ultimate test. Who will be victorious? Put readers in the center of the supermoto action as they learn about everything from race rules to track features and equipment. Carefully leveled, high-energy text helps ensure accessibility for even the most reluctant readers"— Provided by publisher.
Identifiers: LCCN 2024060034 (print) | LCCN 2024060035 (ebook) | ISBN 9798875226250 (hardcover) | ISBN 9798875226205 (paperback) | ISBN 9798875226212 (pdf) | ISBN 9798875226229 (epub) | ISBN 9798875226236 (kindle edition)
Subjects: LCSH: Supermoto—Juvenile literature.
Classification: LCC GV1060.1457 .A47 2026 (print) | LCC GV1060.1457 (ebook) | DDC 796—dc23/eng/20240102
LC record available at https://lccn.loc.gov/2024060034
LC ebook record available at https://lccn.loc.gov/2024060035

Summary: Supermoto racers put their skills to the ultimate test on both pavement and dirt. When the checkered flag waves, one rider will claim victory. Learn about track features, equipment, supermoto stars, and more!

Editorial Credits
Editor: Carrie Sheely; Designer: Dina Her; Media Researcher: Rebekah Hubstenberger; Production Specialist: Tori Abraham

Image Credits
Alamy: K.C. Alfred/SDU-T/ZUMA Press Inc., 19, Kiko Jimenez, 21, 27, 28, Rudmer Zwerver, 11, mauritius images GmbH, 4–5; Getty Images: Christian Petersen, 13, iStock/Hstarr, cover, Rick Loomis/Los Angeles Times, 24; Newscom: Ai Wire - Alan Smith/"Ai Wire Photo Service", 17, 25; Shutterstock: OcMaRUS, 7, 8, 12, 14, 15, 16, 18, 29, SL Chen, 22

Design Credits
Shutterstock: backup, Goromaru, JACKREZNOR, Miloje, salam kerrong

Any additional websites and resources referenced in this book are not maintained, authorized, or sponsored by Capstone. All product and company names are trademarks™ or registered® trademarks of their respective holders.

Printed and bound in China. 006276

TABLE OF CONTENTS

All About Supermoto 6

Getting Ready 10

Race Time! 16

Going Pro 26

    Glossary 30

    Read More 31

    Internet Sites 31

    Index 32

    About the Author 32

Words in **bold** are in the glossary.

WHAT IS SUPERMOTO?

Supermoto is an exciting kind of motorcycle racing. The course has flat dirt sections, paved sections, and jumps.

lightweight frame

strong brakes

SUPERMOTO BIKE DIAGRAM

strong suspension system

powerful engine

wide, smooth tires

5

CHAPTER 1
ALL ABOUT SUPERMOTO

In the late 1970s, Gavin Trippe had a big idea. He wanted to create a TV show. In it, motorcycle racers would compete.

The course would include paved and dirt sections to see who was the best all-around racer. His show, *The Superbikers*, was a hit! With it, supermoto was born.

Supermoto bikes are much like **motocross** bikes, which race only on dirt tracks. But supermoto bikes are lighter. Unlike motocross bikes, they have smooth tires to grip **pavement**.

A supermoto bike needs strong brakes. Supermoto tracks have many tight turns. Riders need to slow down often.

CHAPTER 2
GETTING READY

Race day is near. It's time to get the course ready! A supermoto course is mostly pavement. It has some dirt sections. These may have jumps and corners with **berms**.

Races are often held on go-kart tracks or other racetracks. They may also be in a stadium or parking lot. Dirt is added to the course.

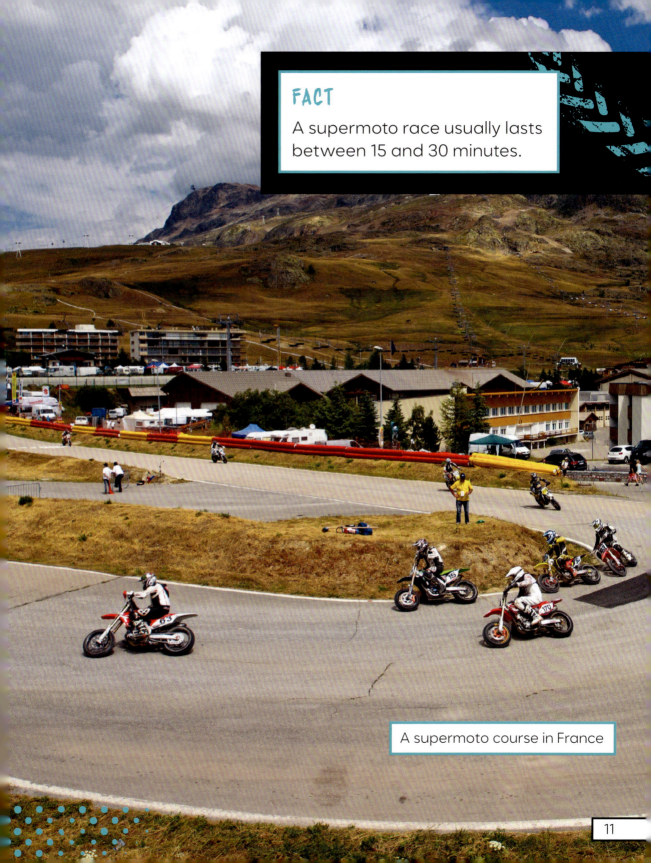

FACT

A supermoto race usually lasts between 15 and 30 minutes.

A supermoto course in France

Supermoto racers train hard. Riders need strength and skill. They spend many hours practicing jumps and turns. Some riders take supermoto training classes. Riders work out and eat healthy foods.

Before a race, riders make sure their bikes are ready. Is the gas in the tank at the right level? Check! Are the tires at the right air **pressure**? Check!

Then riders suit up. Supermoto can be dangerous. Riders wear leather jackets and pants. The jacket includes body armor. Riders also wear helmets, gloves, goggles, and boots.

CHAPTER 3
RACE TIME!

Finally, it's time to race! The racers line up in rows behind the starting line. They rev their engines.

Some events have heat races and qualifiers. Top riders from these races move on.

The starting gate drops. *Zoom*! The riders race to the first turn. Then they speed down a long, straight section. The next turn is sharp! The bikes lean way over. The riders' knees touch the pavement.

A dirt section is next. The racers slow their speed. They skid around corners. A rider spins out. The other riders swerve to miss him. Dust flies!

Next up are jumps. Riders sail up the first one. They land on the downslope of the second jump. Soon they zip through a tunnel. They're back on the pavement.

The riders battle for first place in each **lap**. The first three riders are close to one another. They ride faster on the **straightaways**. They lean even tighter into the corners.

In the back of the pack, some riders crash. The yellow flag waves. This tells other riders that they need to be careful and slow down.

At last the riders reach the finish line. The checkered flag waves. The winners step up on the **podium**. They hold their trophies high.

Winners of a supermoto race in California on the podium

CHAPTER 4
GOING PRO

Both **amateurs** and professionals compete in supermoto. One of the world's largest pro events is the SuperMoto World Championship. Racers battle for the title in the series. Events are held in Belgium, Italy, and other countries.

FACT

The Fédération Internationale de Motocyclisme (FIM) puts on the SuperMoto World Championship. It also hosts world championship series in motocross and other events.

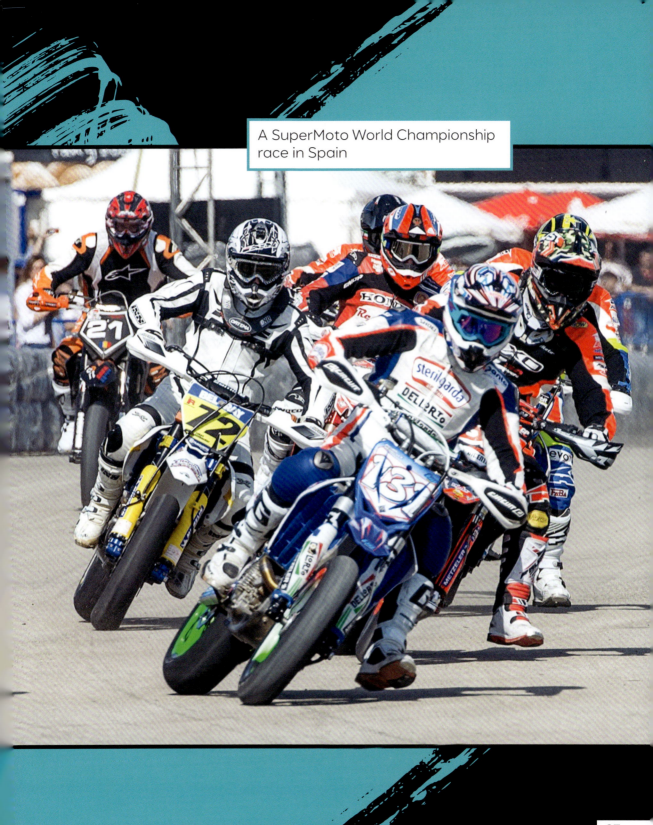

A SuperMoto World Championship race in Spain

27

New supermoto stars are crowned each year. Thomas Chareyre of France is one of the most well-known. He is an eight-time SuperMoto World Championship winner. With each race, riders give their all for the win!

Thomas Chareyre races in Spain.

GLOSSARY

amateur (AM-uh-chur)—an athlete who takes part in a sport for pleasure rather than for money

berm (BURM)—a banked turn or corner on a racetrack

lap (LAP)—one time around a racetrack

pavement (PAYV-muhnt)—the hard surface of a road or track

podium (POH-dee-uhm)—a platform where winners receive their prizes

pressure (PRESH-ur)—the force produced by pushing on something

straightaway (strayt-uh-WAY)—a straight part of a racecourse

READ MORE

Abdo, Kenny. *Motocross*. Minneapolis: Abdo Zoom, 2024.

Conaghan, Bernard. *Motocross*. New York: Crabtree Publishing, 2023.

Kaiser, Brianna. *Supermoto: Rev It Up!* Minneapolis: Lerner Publications, 2023.

INTERNET SITES

American Motorcyclist Association: Supermoto
americanmotorcyclist.com/racing/track-racing/supermoto

FIM Supermoto World Championship S1GP
prev.supermotos1gp.com

Supermoto
topendsports.com/sport/list/motorcycle-supermoto.htm#google_vignette

INDEX

air pressure, 14

brakes, 4, 9

Chareyre, Thomas, 28

courses, 10

crashes, 23

engines, 16

flags, 23, 25

heat races, 17

jumps, 4, 10, 12, 20

laps, 23

podiums, 25

qualifiers, 17

starting gates, 19

straightaways, 23

suiting up, 15

SuperMoto World Championship, 26, 28

tires, 5, 9, 14

training, 12

Trippe, Gavin, 6

turns, 9, 12, 19, 20, 23

ABOUT THE AUTHOR

Lisa J. Amstutz is the author of more than 150 children's books on topics ranging from applesauce to zebra mussels. An ecologist by training, she enjoys sharing her love of nature with kids. Lisa lives on a small farm with her family.